THE
CACAO
COOKBOOK

—

An Hachette UK Company
www.hachette.co.uk

First published in Great Britain in 2018 by Aster, an imprint of
Octopus Publishing Group Ltd, Carmelite House,
50 Victoria Embankment, London EC4Y 0DZ
www.octopus.co.uk

ISBN 978-1-91202-376-9

A CIP catalogue record for this book is available from the
British Library.

Printed and bound in China.

10 9 8 7 6 5 4 3 2 1

Consultant Publisher Kate Adams
Recipe Developer and Food Stylist Nicole Pisani, Food for Happiness
Senior Designer Jaz Bahra
Assistant Editor Nell Warner
Copy Editor Clare Sayer
Photographer Issy Croker
Food and Props Stylist Emily Ezekiel
Production Manager Caroline Alberti

Picture credits: 7 Quagga Media/Alamy Stock Photo; 9 pierivb/iStock;
11 Science History Images/Alamy Stock Photo; 16-17 renacall/iStock

THE
CACAO
COOKBOOK

Discover the health benefits
and uses of cacao, with
50 delicious recipes

CONTENTS

INTRODUCTION

Cacao, or *Theobroma cacao* (Greek for 'food of the gods'), is the source
of original, natural chocolate. Cacao as an ingredient comes from
the seeds of the fruit of the cacao tree and has been revered by the
indigenous peoples of South America, or Mesoamerica (which includes
Mexico, Central America and South America) as far back as 1600 BC.

Before cacao was cultivated as a crop, it was used in rituals including
religious ceremonies, births, marriages and funerals, and as a medicine.
As it became a type of currency, cacao began to be cultivated, especially
by the Mayans around 600 AD.

Columbus was the first European to come across cacao in 1502, and a
couple of decades after this initial discovery, Cortez then recorded the
use of cacao in the court of Emperor Montezuma.

It would be 1657 before the first hot chocolate shop was opened in
London, and in the US Baker's Chocolate was founded in 1780, producers
of the type of chocolate we are familiar with in the modern day.

There are three main varieties of cocoa bean used in the production
of chocolate or cacao products.

Forastero
This high-yield variety of the cacao tree represents the majority of the
world's total cocoa production. *Forastero* means 'stranger' or 'outsider'
in Spanish. It is found in Ghana, Nigeria, Ivory Coast, New Guinea, Brazil,
Central America, Sri Lanka, Malaysia and Indonesia.

Criollo
This is a higher quality and less-bitter cocoa bean than forastero – and
so tends to be used to make higher quality chocolate. This explains why
single-origin chocolate produced from criollo beans is so sought-after
(and expensive), especially as it is also quite rare. It is found in Venezuela,
Mexico, Nicaragua, Guatemala, Colombia, Samoan Islands, Sri Lanka
and Madagascar.

Trinitario

Forastero beans were cross-fertilized with criollo beans in Trinidad after the hurricane of 1727 destroyed the plantations. These are therefore found mainly in the Caribbean but also in Venezuela and Colombia.

The large rugby-ball like pods that grow on cacao trees are harvested and cracked open to release the cacao beans. The beans are covered with banana leaves and placed in a type of wooden bin or pit in the ground to ferment – this begins the transformation of the beans from their extremely bitter natural state into the main ingredient for chocolate. After fermentation, the beans are then dried in the sun before being transported to the manufacturer for processing.

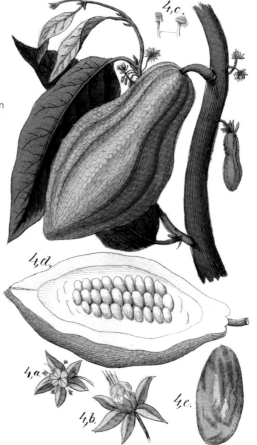

Right: Theobroma Cacao.

Cacao versus cocoa

Cacao and cocoa both come from the cocoa bean, the difference is in the amount of processing. Cacao is made by cold-pressing unroasted cacao beans, whereas cocoa is raw cacao that has been roasted at high temperatures; it is then usually sweetened with sugar. Cocoa still has many of the nutrients that cacao has (*see* page 14–15), just in smaller quantities due to the heat in the processing.

The different types of cacao

Once cacao beans are dried, they are then cold-pressed to remove the cacao butter, the fatty part of the fruit found in the inner part of the lining of the bean. The beans are then either ground to create raw cacao powder or crushed to create the nibs. Solid cacao is a combination of the raw cacao powder and cacao butter:

- **Cacao powder** has a bitter chocolaty taste.
- **Cacao nibs** are similar to chocolate chips but are more bitter and 'savoury' in taste.
- **Solid (100%) cacao chocolate** is an extremely dark, quite bitter chocolate with no sugar added, made by combining raw cacao powder and cacao butter.
- **Cacao butter** is white in colour and is buttery and chocolaty in texture – it has an incredible aroma of chocolate. It's used to make chocolate and natural beauty products (*see* pages 96 and 116–125).

Opposite: Cacao pods from Madagascar.

CACAO TRADITIONS: FOOD OF THE GODS

Cacao was part of the Mayan creation myth, Popol Vuh. It was one of the ingredients, along with corn, used by the gods to make the first humans, made by the gods so that they would be worshipped by them. To the Mayans, therefore, cacao was in the essence of humanity, and so it became a ceremonial elixir. Due to its aphrodisiac qualities (it contains Tryptophan, a building block of serotonin, and phenylethylamine, a part of amphetamine, which are both associated with good mood and feelings of falling in love), Maya couples would drink cacao at engagement and marriage ceremonies.

Archaeological vessels found in tombs from the Mesoamerican period also found cacao cooked with turkey and fish, suggesting that cacao was originally considered to be a savoury rather than sweet ingredient, which makes sense when you taste raw cacao. It was the Spanish who began to serve cacao as a hot and sweet drink, and in the 1700s, when hot cacao hit London, cacao houses popped up just as artisan coffee shops are in abundance today.

Aztec mythology
In Aztec mythology, the god named Quetzalcoatl brought down the cacao tree from heaven to earth. This is why the drink made from dried and fermented cacao beans was thought to bring wisdom.

The Aztecs drank cacao cold, made with corn, chilli and vanilla. Achiote, another spice, was used to give the cacao drink a red colour.

Opposite: A depiction of the Aztec god Xiuhtecuhtli from The Codex Fejérváry-Mayer, 15th century.

THE CACAO CEREMONY

According to Rebekah Shaman, who gives shamanic guidance and offers ceremonial events including cacao ceremonies, cacao is also a powerful plant medicine that has been used in ceremonies for millennia across Central and South America, especially by the Mayan people, who believed that cacao was discovered by the gods. The word 'cacao' itself originates from the Maya words *kak'au* and *chokola'j*, which combine to mean 'to drink chocolate

'Cacao has many amazing, life-affirming qualities that support health and psychological well-being. She is a powerful Plant Medicine that helps us to release emotional blockages that no longer serve us, find forgiveness in ourselves and others, and shows us the way forward if we are stuck, or afraid of making necessary life changes. It also enables us to access stuck emotions, conditionings, patterns of behaviour and addictions that are buried deep in the unconscious.'
—Rebekah Shaman

The cacao ceremony, now becoming more popular across the world, is thought to create a euphoric state in which the release of negative energy, connection with heart energy and personal or spiritual transformation may take place. Ceremonies will vary in their approach, depending on the shaman conducting the ceremony. They usually take place in a circle with prayer, sharing intention and the cacao is served as a drink. Ceremonial grade cacao is used and it is often mixed with water, chilli and honey or other herbs.

THE HEALTH BENEFITS OF CACAO

It's official. Chocolate is good for us. Or rather, raw, cold-processed cacao is particularly good for us. Cacao powder, or nibs, are healthier than cocoa powder as all the natural nutrients of the cacao bean are retained, so it has naturally high levels of flavanols, fibre and protein. Cacao is also said to be one of the highest sources of antioxidants of all foods. Raw cacao contains a number of beneficial minerals and chemicals that are good for our health, from helping to balance blood sugar, to maintaining heart health, brain health and healthy weight loss.

ANTIOXIDANTS
Raw cacao contains over 40 times the antioxidants of blueberries. Antioxidants absorb the free radicals that we are exposed to from pollution and toxins in our environment, causing cell and tissue damage and often leading to diseases such as cancer.

IRON
Cacao is the highest plant-based source of iron with 7.3mg per 100g (in comparison spinach has 3.6mg per 100g). As is the case with all plant-based iron, it is best combined with vitamin C to aid absorption into the body.

MAGNESIUM
Cacao is also a plant-based source of magnesium, which is needed for optimum muscle and nerve function.

CALCIUM
Although it's unlikely that you would consume 100g raw cacao instead of drinking 100ml cow's milk, it is worth noting that cacao contains 160mg calcium per 100g compared to 125mg per 100ml milk.

MOOD BOOSTER

Cacao is a source of both serotonin and tryptophan, two of the key 'good mood' chemicals. It also triggers the release of dopamine and endorphins, thanks to phenylethylamine and anandamide, also known as the 'bliss molecule'. These chemicals help to relieve emotional stress and produce a natural sense of pleasure.

FIBRE AND MUFA

Cacao is also a good source of fibre and monounsaturated fats or MUFAs, the healthy fats that keep you fuller for longer and help to lower cholesterol and reduce the risk of heart disease and stroke.

IF YOU ARE SENSITIVE TO CAFFEINE

Cacao beans contain theobromine, which is a nervous system stimulant that has a similar effect to caffeine; it's the ingredient that makes chocolate unsafe for dogs. If you are sensitive to caffeine then you will want to be careful how much, if any, cacao you consume.

Next page: Cacao pods
on a tree, Brazil.

COOKING WITH CACAO

We tend to think of desserts and baking when we first think of cacao or cocoa, and especially when we think of chocolate. However, because raw cacao is unsweetened, it works well in savoury dishes as well as sweet, and chefs and flavour experts suggest that it works particularly well with spices, especially chilli, cardamom, wasabi, clove and cinnamon. It can be paired with meats including beef, pork, steak, venison and duck, as well as shellfish, beetroot and certain cheeses, including ricotta and Parmesan. That is why you will find some slightly unusual sounding combinations in this collection of cacao recipes.

Here are some of the ways in which you can use the different types of cacao in your cooking:

- Add a few shavings of solid cacao to stews to add a wonderful extra layer of flavour.
- Use the nibs as a healthy alternative to chocolate chips, perfect for your morning porridge. They are often toasted to boost the flavour (see opposite).
- Add a spoonful of cacao powder to your favourite smoothie for an extra hit of antioxidants.
- Make your own chocolate with cacao butter.
- Break off a square of solid cacao chocolate to make a healthy hot chocolate drink.

The majority of the recipes in this book avoid cooking cacao at high temperatures as heat affects the nutrient content, although we couldn't resist a classic brownie recipe, with a few chia seeds thrown into the mix. There are also a few variations of some classic cacao recipes from around the world, including the Mexican mole and hot cacao, picada sauce from Spain and 'chocolate salami'

TOASTED CACAO NIBS

If you haven't tasted a raw cacao nib and you imagine they taste anything like what we know of as 'chocolate', think again! As they contain no sugar, nibs are quite bitter. One easy way to boost the flavour of cacao nibs is to toast them.

- Preheat the oven to 180°C (350°F), Gas Mark 4.

- Spread the cacao nibs out on a baking tray and bake for 10 minutes.

- Remove from the oven and cool completely before using.

- Store in an airtight container.

DRINKS

◇◇◇◇◇◇

HOT CACAO

In South America you'll find an amazing variety of hot chocolate recipes, among them *tascalate* (or *tazcalate*), which is made with ground roasted corn, chocolate, ground pine nuts, achiote, vanilla and sugar. All the ingredients are ground together, mixed with milk and heated; for a cold drink the ingredients are stirred into cold water and added to ice. Another tradition is to add chilli to hot chocolate. Here, we have combined the antioxidants of cacao with turmeric, famed for its anti-inflammatory properties. The coconut oil helps to emulsify the raw cacao so that you get a silky consistency.

400ml almond milk

1 tablespoon coconut oil

1 tablespoon cacao powder

½ teaspoon raw maca powder

½ teaspoon ground turmeric

3 pinches of ground cinnamon

pinch of cayenne

pinch of sea salt

Heat the almond milk and coconut oil in a saucepan. Mix a little of the warm milk with the rest of the ingredients to form a smooth, loose paste. Add this to the rest of the milk and whisk to combine all the ingredients before serving.

TONIC

This is a wonderfully refreshing and light drink. If you can find blood orange juice, the colour is intense, although any citrus juice will work well with this recipe.

1 teaspoon cacao powder

1 teaspoon maple syrup

juice of an orange

250ml blood orange juice
(or orange juice)

500ml tonic water

Make a paste with the cacao powder, maple syrup and juice of an orange. Mix into the the blood orange juice and tonic water and serve over plenty of ice.

ACAI CACAO SMOOTHIE

Acai smoothies have become a famous export from Brazil – the palm trees from which the berries are harvested are mostly native to Central and South America. Acai and cacao are a classic, luxurious combination.

---

1 tablespoon acai berry powder

1 tablespoon cacao powder

1 frozen banana, sliced

generous handful of frozen blueberries

1 tablespoon almond butter (optional)

1 tablespoon ground flaxseeds

150ml almond milk, plus extra if needed

Put all the ingredients into a blender and blitz until smooth.

Add a little more almond milk if you like a thinner consistency.

CACAO MATCHA SMOOTHIE

Matcha is another amazing source of antioxidants, while avocado adds healthy monounsaturated fats to this smoothie, so that you will feel fuller for longer. We have also included kefir in this recipe, a type of fermented milk that is packed with beneficial bacteria, but if you don't have this to hand you can use any type of nut milk or some apple juice instead.

½ frozen banana, sliced
1 tablespoon cacao powder
1 teaspoon matcha powder
handful of spinach
½ ripe avocado, peeled
    and stoned
100ml kefir

Put all the ingredients into a blender and blitz until smooth.

Add a little water if you prefer a thinner consistency.

PEANUT BUTTER CHIA

This high-protein smoothie will power up your morning
and the peanut butter will really keep you going, especially
after a workout.

1 tablespoon peanut butter

2 tablespoons natural yogurt

1 tablespoon soaked chia seeds
(1 teaspoon dry seeds soaked
overnight in 4 tablespoons
water)

½ frozen banana, sliced (or use
3 tablespoons frozen berries)

1 tablespoon cacao powder

150ml coconut milk

Put all the ingredients into a blender and blitz
until smooth.

BREAKFASTS

PORRIDGE OF THE GODS

The pumpkin in this recipe might not sound like a natural breakfast
ingredient, but believe us when we say this is delicious, especially with
the flavours of maple syrup, cacao, clove and cinnamon.

50g porridge oats (use gluten-free
   oats if you are intolerant)
100ml milk of choice
1 tablespoon pumpkin purée
1 tablespoon maple syrup or
   clear honey
¼ teaspoon ground cinnamon
1 teaspoon cacao powder
pinch of ground cloves
1 tablespoon natural yogurt or
   dairy-free coconut yogurt
a few pieces dried mango
1 tablespoon Cacao Nuts and
   Seeds (see page 57)

Place the oats, milk and 100ml water to a saucepan and
bring to the boil.

Reduce the heat to a simmer and stir in the pumpkin
purée, maple syrup or honey, cinnamon, cacao powder
and cloves.

Simmer gently for about 10 minutes, stirring every now
and then, until the oats are soft.

Leave to stand for a couple of minutes before serving
with a spoonful of yogurt, dried mango and some Cacao
Nuts and Seeds.

GRANOLA

Whenever we make a batch of granola, we wonder why we don't do it all the time as it's so easy; it's also difficult to make a bad flavour combination choice when it comes to granola. So if you have almonds instead of hazelnuts, go ahead and use almonds, likewise if you have a packet of dried apricots you want to use up, swap those in for the dried berries.

250g jumbo oats

150g hazelnuts, roughly chopped

50g pumpkin seeds

2 tablespoons cacao powder

2 heaped tablespoons coconut oil
(when solid)

60g maple syrup

1 teaspoon vanilla extract

100g dried blueberries or
cranberries

2 tablespoons cacao nibs

Preheat the oven to 140°C (275°F), Gas Mark 1 and line a large baking tray with baking paper.

Mix the oats, nuts, seeds and cacao powder together in a large bowl.

Heat the coconut oil and maple syrup in a small saucepan until dissolved, and mix in the vanilla extract. Pour this into the dry ingredients and stir thoroughly so that all the oats, nuts and seeds are evenly coated.

Pour the granola on to the baking paper and spread out evenly. Bake for about 45 minutes, then sprinkle over the dried berries and cacao nibs and bake for another 10–15 minutes.

Leave to cool and then gently bring up the sides of the paper to transfer the granola to a large airtight jar.

OVERNIGHT OATS

Soaking oats overnight means that you have a quick base for a delicious breakfast the next morning. This recipe is based on a Bircher muesli, which is traditionally served cold, but equally you could heat up the oats for a warming porridge.

50g porridge oats (use gluten-free
    oats if you are intolerant)
1 teaspoon flaxseeds
1 teaspoon chia seeds
1 tablespoon cacao powder
150ml almond milk (or milk of
    choice)
1 tablespoon maple syrup
    (optional)
3 drops of vanilla extract

To serve
juice of ½ lime
2 tablespoons natural yogurt
    (or dairy-free coconut yogurt)
½ apple, chopped
1 tablespoon roughly chopped
    almonds
1 teaspoon toasted cacao nibs
(*see* page 19)

Combine all the dry ingredients in a large bowl and then add the almond milk, maple syrup (if using) and vanilla extract and stir thoroughly. Transfer to an airtight glass container and leave to soften overnight.

To serve, stir through the lime juice, yogurt, chopped apple and almonds. Finish by scattering over the toasted cacao nibs.

BRAN MUFFINS

The blackstrap molasses and cacao powder make these muffins not for the faint-hearted, and are dark, bittersweet and delicious warm with a little extra butter.

100g wheat bran

150g raisins

100g spelt flour

1 tablespoon cacao powder

1 teaspoon baking powder

1 teaspoon bicarbonate of soda

1 teaspoon sea salt

75g butter

50g coconut sugar

2 tablespoons blackstrap molasses

2 tablespoons clear honey

1 teaspoon vanilla extract

2 eggs

250g Greek yogurt

Preheat the oven to 180°C (350°F), Gas Mark 4 and line a large baking sheet (or two) with baking paper. Line large 6-cup muffin tray (or a regular 12-cup muffin tray) with paper cases.

Spread the wheat bran out evenly across the lined baking sheet and toast in the oven for 10 minutes, checking to make sure it doesn't burn. Set aside to cool.

Put the raisins and 200ml water into a saucepan and simmer over a low heat until all the water has been absorbed by the raisins. Remove the raisins from the pan and set aside to cool.

Sift the flour into a bowl and mix through the cacao powder, baking powder, bicarbonate of soda and salt. Use a hand-held electric whisk to cream together the butter and sugar in a separate bowl, until fluffy. Add the molasses, honey and vanilla and whisk again until just combined. Add the egg and whisk briefly until just incorporated. Add the yogurt and drained raisins and mix until just combined.

Add the dry ingredients to the wet and mix together until combined to make a batter. Pour the batter into the paper cases and bake in the oven for 20–25 minutes, or until a skewer pierced in the centre of the muffins comes out clean. Larger muffins will take a little longer. Transfer the muffins to a wire rack to cool completely.

GINGER AND CACAO BISCOTTI

Perfect for dipping in a cup of hot cacao or coffee, the best thing about making your own biscotti is that you can decide what size you want to make them. Also, we like to bake them just a little softer than regular biscotti.

1 large egg

60g coconut sugar

120g plain flour, plus extra
   for dusting

½ teaspoon baking powder

1 teaspoon ground ginger

½ teaspoon ground turmeric

50g cacao drops

Preheat the oven to 170°C (340°F) Gas Mark 3½ and lightly grease a baking tray.

Whisk the egg and sugar with a hand-held electric mixer for about 5 minutes until frothy and leaving 'ribbon' trails in the mixture.

Add the dry ingredients and combine thoroughly to form a sticky ball of dough. Lightly dust your hands with flour and then work the dough into a log about 30cm long. Place the log on to the baking tray, flatten slightly and bake in the oven for 20 minutes.

Remove from the oven and cut the log into 1cm slices. Place each biscotti back on to the baking tray and return to the oven for 8–10 minutes, or until golden.

Leave the biscotti to cool completely. You can eat them immediately or store in an airtight container for about a week.

PROTEIN BREAKFAST BARS

These breakfast bars are perfect to make for a busy week ahead, packing in plenty of nutrients. The seeds are the star of the show here, and we've added beetroot powder as it goes brilliantly with the cacao, but you could try also try using matcha powder.

100g pumpkin seeds

80g flaxseeds

180g soft pitted dates

120g soft dried apricots

2 tablespoons extra virgin coconut oil

1 tablespoon cacao powder

1 tablespoon beetroot powder

pinch of sea salt

50g melted cacao (optional)

Line a small baking tin with baking paper.

Place the pumpkin seeds in a food processor and grind just for a couple of seconds. Pour the chopped seeds into a large mixing bowl and combine with the flaxseeds.

Put the dates, apricots and coconut oil into the food processor and process until you have a paste. Combine the date paste with the seeds and add the cacao powder, beetroot powder, if using, and sea salt and stir until the mixture sticks together.

Press the mixture into a the prepared tin, then place in the freezer for at least 2–3 hours. Remove from the tin and peel off the paper. Cut into small bars and drizzle over the melted cacao, if using.

The bars will keep in the refrigerator in an airtight container for up to a month, ready to eat whenever you need one.

CACAO BRAZIL NUT BUTTER

This recipe would work equally well with hazelnuts, peanuts, almonds or cashew nuts. Or for a really simple option, simply stir some cacao powder and coconut syrup or agave nectar through your nut butter of choice.

400g Brazil nuts

2 tablespoons cacao powder

3 tablespoons avocado oil

6 tablespoons coconut syrup or
   agave nectar

pinch of sea salt

1 tablespoon chopped pistachios

1 tablespoon pine nuts

Blend all the ingredients, except the chopped pistachios and pine nuts, together in a food processor or high-speed blender in bursts of about 30 seconds. Keep going for 8–10 minutes until the oil releases and a smooth paste forms. You will need to scrape down the sides of the bowl or blender a few times.

Stir through the pistachios and pine nuts.

Transfer to an airtight container and keep in the refrigerator for up to a month.

Serve on toast with a little honey drizzled over.

GRILLED CHEESE AND CACAO RELISH

According to flavour experts, chocolate and cheese make an unusual but excellent flavour pairing. We've added cacao to a tomato relish for a sweet and savoury combination that perks up any cheese toastie.

4 slices of rye bread
20g unsalted butter
100g Comté cheese, grated
80g baby spinach
sea salt

For the relish
10g butter
1 small onion, diced
2 tomatoes, diced
10g cacao nibs
½ teaspoon dried chilli flakes
pinch of sea salt
1 tablespoon coconut sugar

To make the relish, place a nonstick pan over a low-medium heat and add the butter. When bubbling, add the onion, tomatoes, cacao nibs, chilli flakes and salt and sauté for 10 minutes until soft. Stir through the coconut sugar and continue to heat the chutney until it becomes sticky, another 10 minutes or so. Take off the heat and leave to cool while you make the cheese toast.

Preheat the grill and place a griddle pan over a medium heat while you butter the slices of bread on both sides. Griddle the bread until toasted on each side.

Pile grated cheese on to each slice of toast, reserving a little to serve, and place under the grill until melted and bubbling.

Melt the remaining butter in a saucepan and wilt the baby spinach in a pan with a pinch of sea salt.

To make your toasties, put half the remaining grated cheese on to one of the cheese toasts. Add a spoonful of relish and some spinach, and top with another cheese toast. Repeat to make a second toastie and devour with a friend.

TURKISH EGGS

We tried adding a little cacao to the traditional Turkish recipe for poached eggs and yogurt – the bitter chocolate works brilliantly with the chilli oil. This is something a bit special for the weekend.

---

splash of white wine vinegar,
    for poaching
4 eggs
200g natural yogurt
1 tablespoon chilli oil
½ teaspoon dried chilli flakes
1 tablepoon cacao nibs
½ teaspoon sea salt flakes
4 slices of toasted sourdough,
    to serve
mustard cress, to serve (optional)

Bring a large saucepan of water to the boil and add a small splash of white wine vinegar. Crack each egg into individual ramekins or small bowls. Stir the water vigorously in one direction and then gently tip the eggs one by one into the middle of the water. Poach for 3 minutes, then remove with a slotted spoon and drain on kitchen paper.

Divide the yogurt between your serving bowls. Top the yogurt with the poached eggs and a drizzle of chilli oil. Garnish with dried chilli flakes and cacao nibs and scatter over a little sea salt.

Serve with toasted sourdough to dip into the eggs and yogurt, and some mustard cress, if using.

HOMEMADE BAKED BEANS

These beans are delicious and make a protein-packed fulfilling breakfast, lunch or light supper. You could also top with an egg for Sunday brunch.

2 tablespoons olive oil
80g onion, finely diced
80g carrots, finely diced
½ celery stick, finely diced
1 tablespoon tomato purée
1 bay leaf
3 sprigs of thyme, leaves picked
300ml passata
¼ teaspoon mustard powder
¼ teaspoon ground cloves
2 teaspoons cacao powder
1 tablespoon maple syrup
150ml hot vegetable stock
800g tinned cannellini beans
Toasted brioche (or any type
    of toast) and grilled bacon,
    to serve

Heat the olive oil in a large lidded casserole and sauté the onion, carrots and celery for about 10 minutes over a low-medium heat. Stir in the tomato purée, herbs, passata, spices, cacao and maple syrup. Add the stock, bring to the boil and then reduce to a simmer and cook for 20 minutes.

Preheat the oven to 180°C (350°F), Gas Mark 4.

Add the beans, stir through, put on the lid and cook in the oven for 20 minutes to combine all the flavours.

Serve on toast with grilled bacon, if liked.

SOUPS & SIDES

SQUASH, CASHEW NUT AND CACAO SOUP

The natural sweetness of the butternut squash brings out the flavour of the cacao in this soup. Chilli and cacao are natural partners in South America; here just a hint of a kick brings everything together. We have served it chilled, but it is equally delicious when warmed.

1 tablespoon groundnut oil

1 small onion, peeled and sliced

500g butternut squash (unpeeled weight), peeled and roughly chopped

1 carrot, sliced

2 teaspoons cacao nibs

1 teaspoon mild chilli powder

½ teaspoon sea salt

500ml hot vegetable stock

1 tablespoon cashew nut butter

mixed cress or baby leaves, to serve

Heat the oil in a heavy-based saucepan, add the onion and sauté for about 10 minutes until translucent. Add the squash and carrot and then stir in the cacao nibs, chilli powder and salt, continuing to sauté for a few more minutes to allow the flavours to infuse.

Add the hot stock and bring to the boil, then reduce to a simmer and cook for 15 minutes, or until all the vegetables are tender. Stir through the cashew nut butter, leave to cool a little and then blitz in a blender until smooth.

Chill in the refrigerator for about an hour.

Serve chilled, scattered with cress or baby leaves.

CAULIFLOWER SOUP
WITH CACAO BUCKWHEAT

The cauliflower soup base in this recipe is classic, light and smooth, so the textures and flavours of the roasted cauliflower, cacao and roasted buckwheat add a wonderful edge, both visually and in terms of taste. This is so good!

4 tablespoons olive oil

3 banana shallots, sliced

2 garlic cloves, thinly sliced

2 bay leaves

2 teaspoons thyme leaves

½ teaspoon sea salt

100ml dry white wine

1 medium-large cauliflower

500ml hot vegetable stock

2 teaspoons rosemary leaves

1 tablespoon cacao nibs

1 tablespoon clear honey or
    maple syrup

2 tablespoons roasted buckwheat

Heat 2 tablespoons of the olive oil in a heavy-based saucepan and add the shallots and garlic. Soften gently over a low heat for 5 minutes and then add the bay leaves, thyme and salt. After a few more minutes, increase the heat and add the wine to the pan.

Remove the outer leaves from the cauliflower and reserve about a quarter of the cauliflower. Roughly chop the rest and add this to the pan once the wine has reduced by half. Stir through and sauté the cauliflower for about 5 minutes before adding the hot stock. Bring to the boil, then reduce to a simmer and cook for about 10 minutes until the cauliflower is easily pierced with a sharp knife. Remove the bay leaves. Leave to cool a little before blending to a smooth soup.

To make the garnish, break the remaining cauliflower into florets and slice them. Place a nonstick pan over a medium heat and add the remaining olive oil. When hot, add the sliced cauliflower and sauté for a minute before adding the rosemary and cacao nibs. Continue to sauté for another minute or so until the cauliflower is tender. Add the honey and stir through, then add the buckwheat, stirring to combine.

Ladle the hot soup into bowls and top with the rosemary and cacao cauliflower and buckwheat.

SERVES 6
◇◇◇◇◇◇

CACAO CHEESE STRAWS
WITH SPICED YOGURT

These cheese straws are so moreish and are perfect for celebrations
and gatherings. Apparently wasabi is a good flavour companion for
cacao and so we decided to add a little of both here. The spiced yogurt
would also make a great dip for raw vegetables.

For the spiced yogurt
1 green chilli, deseeded and finely
   chopped
1 teaspoon finely chopped mint
   leaves, plus extra to serve
1 teaspoon snipped chives, plus
   extra to serve
1 garlic clove, finely grated
½ teaspoon ground cumin
½ teaspoon ground cardamom
½ teaspoon ground coriander
250g Greek yogurt
1 teaspoon cacao nibs
1 teaspoon toasted buckwheat
1 teaspoon chopped hazelnuts
extra virgin olive oil

For the cheese straws
375g sheet of ready-rolled
   shortcrust pastry
50g grated Cheddar cheese
pinch of wasabi or mustard powder
1 teaspoon cacao powder
1 egg, beaten

For the spiced yogurt, mix together the chilli, herbs,
garlic, spices and yogurt, and leave to sit for at least
1 hour (20 minutes at room temperature and then
40 minutes in the refrigerator) to bring all of the
flavours together.

Preheat the oven to 200°C (400°F), Gas Mark 6 and line
a baking tray with baking paper.

Unroll the pastry sheet and cover one half with the
grated Cheddar, wasabi or mustard powder and cacao
powder. Fold the pastry over like a book and roll lightly
with a rolling pin to seal. Cut the pastry into 1cm strips,
then halve each strip and twist 2–3 times. Place each
pastry straw on the lined baking tray.

Brush the pastry straws with beaten egg and bake in
the oven for 25–30 minutes, or until golden and crisp.
Place the chilled yogurt in a bowl and top with some
herbs, cacao nibs, toasted buckwheat, hazelnuts and a
drizzle of olive oil. Serve alongside the cheese straws
for dipping.

CACAO NUTS AND SEEDS

Nuts and seeds are packed with goodness, and this simple recipe adds
a wonderful bittersweet crunch against the nuttiness.

100g raw almonds

100g raw cashews

100g pumpkin seeds

50g unsweetened desiccated
    coconut

3 tablespoons cacao powder

1 tablespoon rosemary, finely
    chopped

1 teaspoon sea salt

60ml olive oil

30ml maple syrup

20g coconut sugar

Preheat the oven to 180°C (350°F), Gas Mark 4.

Spread the almonds and cashews out evenly on a
baking tray and toast for 5 minutes. Remove from oven
and shake the pan a little to help the almonds roast
evenly. Add the pumpkin seeds to the tray and bake for
a further 5 minutes, shaking lightly to make sure they
are evenly toasted.

Remove from the oven and leave to cool for a couple of
minutes before tipping into a bowl. Stir in the coconut,
then add the cacao powder, rosemary and salt and mix
thoroughly.

In a small saucepan, combine together the olive oil,
maple syrup and coconut sugar. Heat gently and once
melted together, pour over the nuts and seeds, stirring
to evenly coat in the liquid.

Spread out the coated nuts and seeds on the baking
tray and bake for another 10–15 minutes. Leave to fully
cool on the tray before transferring to an airtight jar.
These will stay crunchy for up to a week.

ROAST CAULIFLOWER
WITH CACAO AND PAPRIKA BUTTER

Roasting cauliflower whole is not only a great way to present this humble vegetable as a
sharing dish, but it seems to become sweeter in flavour. We have combined cacao with
paprika to make a butter to finish the cauliflower with – sweeter and milder than chilli –
and this dish is delicious served with fish or simply with a grain like quinoa.

1 cauliflower
2 tablespoons olive oil
40g unsalted butter
1 teaspoon sweet smoked paprika
1 teaspoon cacao powder
1 tablespoon cacao nibs
1 tablespoon roasted buckwheat
1 tablespoon chopped hazelnuts
sea salt
handful of leek flowers (optional)

Preheat the oven to 220°C (425°F), Gas Mark 7.

Remove some of the outer leaves of the cauliflower
and cut the bottom so that it sits flat in a roasting tray.
Drizzle over the olive oil and season with salt. Cover it
with foil and roast for about an hour in the oven,
removing the foil after 30 minutes.

Melt the butter in a small saucepan and add the paprika
and cacao powder. Leave the spices to cook a little in the
butter for a couple of minutes so the flavours can infuse.

Serve the cauliflower with the melted butter poured
over and scatter with cacao nibs, roasted buckwheat and
chopped hazelnuts. Season generously and garnish with
leek flowers, if using.

BURRATA
WITH CLEMENTINE AND CACAO NIBS

This is the simplest of recipes that has all the wow factor you need to have
friends coming back for more every time.

1 tablespoon cacao nibs
½ teaspoon dried chilli flakes
1 teaspoon coriander seeds
2 slices sourdough, torn into
 croûtons
4 tablespoons extra virgin olive oil
80g corn salad (or any salad leaves)
20g pea shoots (optional)
2 clementines, peeled and
 segmented
2 burratas, torn into pieces
sea salt

Put the cacao nibs and coriander seeds into a dry frying
pan and toast for a minute or two over a low-medium
heat. Tip out of the pan and leave to cool.

To make the sourdough croûtons, preheat the oven to
200°C (400°F), Gas Mark 6 and line a baking tray with
baking paper. Toss the sourdough pieces in half the
olive oil and spread out on the baking paper. Bake for
10 minutes until crisp.

Arrange the leaves, clementine segments and burrata
pieces in a large shallow serving dish.

Generously drizzle over the remaining extra virgin olive
oil and scatter over toasted coriander seeds, chilli flakes
and cacao nibs. Add a scattering of sea salt and serve with
plenty of crispy sourdough croûtons.

CARDAMOM ROASTED
SWEET POTATO WITH CACAO
AND POMEGRANATE MOLASSES

These sweet potatoes are spicy, sweet and nutty against the cool
soured cream and chives. This recipe is such a simple way to add
amazing flavours to humble vegetables.

2 large sweet potatoes (about
200g), halved
1 teaspoon ground cardamom
pinch of sea salt
2 tablespoons olive oil
1 tablespoon pomegranate
molasses
1 tablespoon cacao nibs
2 tablespoons soured cream
1 tablespoon finely chopped
chives

Preheat the oven to 200°C (400°F), Gas Mark 6.

Mix all the ingredients except the cacao nibs, soured
cream and chives, in a large bowl – making sure the
sweet potatoes are evenly coated with the spices, olive
oil and molasses.

Spread out on a baking tray and bake for about 30
minutes, turning halfway through, until soft on the
inside and caramelized on the outside. Add the cacao
nibs for the last 5 minutes.

Serve with a generous spoonful of soured cream and a
scattering of chives.

BABY KALE AND QUINOA SALAD
WITH FETA AND LIME CACAO DRESSING

This is a lovely fresh salad with protein-packed quinoa, heritage tomatoes and a zesty dressing. You can use any combination of salad vegetables you fancy, for example adding some chopped avocado or new-season asparagus.

100g black quinoa (or use any type of quinoa), rinsed and soaked in water for 30 minutes

100g mixed heritage tomatoes, halved or quartered

80g baby kale

50g feta, crumbled

handful of mint leaves, roughly chopped

4 tablespoons extra virgin olive oil

juice of ½ lime

½ tablespoon cacao nibs

sea salt

Drain and rinse the quinoa, then add to a saucepan with about 300ml cold water. Bring to the boil, then reduce the heat and simmer for 12–15 minutes, or until the water has evaporated. Drain thoroughly.

Gently mix the cooked quinoa with the tomatoes, baby kale, crumbled feta and half the chopped mint.

Make a dressing by whisking together the olive oil, lime juice, cacao nibs and a good pinch of sea salt. Add this to the bowl, gently tossing the salad to distribute the dressing evenly. Taste and adjust the seasoning with more salt or lime juice.

Divide between two shallow bowls and scatter over the remaining mint.

MAIN DISHES

BLACK BEAN AND CORN CHILLI SHAKSHUKA

This hearty veg chilli is packed with flavours and will warm up any
weekday supper. Adjust the levels of heat to suit your taste.

2 teaspoons extra virgin olive oil
1 small onion, finely diced
2 garlic cloves, finely grated
1 tablespoon mild chilli powder
2 teaspoons ground cumin
¼ teaspoon chipotle chilli powder
1 tablespoon cacao nibs
pinch of salt, or to taste
400g can black beans, drained
    and rinsed
150g canned chickpeas, drained
    and rinsed
400g can chopped tomatoes
2 teaspoons lime juice
3 eggs
½ tablespoon olive oil
50g sweetcorn, drained or frozen
sea salt and black pepper
2 spring onions, finely sliced,
    to serve
coriander, to serve

Preheat the oven to 180°C (350°F), Gas Mark 4.

Heat the oil in a shallow ovenproof saucepan (in
which you will serve the dish) over a medium-high
heat. Add the onion and and cook for about 5 minutes,
stirring often, until the onion is slightly softened.

Add the garlic, spices, cacao nibs and salt and cook for
about 30 seconds, stirring constantly, until fragrant.
Add the black beans, chickpeas, tomatoes, 300ml water
and lime juice. Bring to the boil, then cover, reduce the
heat to a gentle simmer and cook for about 20 minutes.
Checking if some water is needed.

Crack the eggs into the pan and transfer to the oven
for 15 minutes or until the eggs are cooked but with
soft yolks.

Heat a griddle pan, add a little olive oil and griddle the
sweetcorn.

Bring the pan to the table and serve scattered with
plenty of freshly ground black pepper, a little sea salt,
sweetcorn, spring onion and lots of fresh coriander.

AVOCADO PRAWN TORTILLAS
WITH BLOOD ORANGE CACAO VINAIGRETTE

This recipe is wonderful for having friends or family around and putting all
the elements in the middle of the table so that you can make your own tacos.

1 medium avocado

juice of ½ lime (about
  1 tablespoon)

½ teaspoon sea salt

½ red chilli, deseeded and finely
  chopped

1 tablespoon olive oil

200g raw and peeled tiger prawns

For the dressing

½ tablespoon cacao nibs

juice of 1 blood orange

1 teaspoon cacao powder

½ teaspoon coconut sugar

2 tablespoons avocado or extra
  virgin olive oil

sea salt

To serve

6 corn tortillas, warmed

150g sweetcorn, drained

20g coriander leaves, torn

50g Asian salad leaves or
  mixed leaves

edible flowers, such as violas
  (optional)

lime juice

Halve and de-stone the avocado and scoop the flesh into
a bowl along with the lime juice, salt and chopped chilli.
Mash into a guacamole-type texture.

For the dressing, toast the cacao nibs in a dry frying pan
over a medium heat for about 15 seconds. Mix the blood
orange juice with the cacao powder and coconut sugar,
then pour in the avocado or extra virgin olive oil and
stir gently to combine. Season to taste with a little sea
salt and set aside.

Place a griddle pan over a medium-high heat and add the
olive oil. Season the prawns with sea salt, and when the
griddle pan is very hot, griddle the prawns for just
20–30 seconds on each side until just cooked.

To assemble the tortillas, spread some avocado mix
over each warmed tortilla and then top with one or
two prawns. Scatter over the sweetcorn, coriander,
salad leaves and edible flowers, if using, and drizzle with
the cacao dressing. Squeeze over some extra lime juice.

OCTOPUS
WITH MOLE

Mole, from the Aztec word *molli*, meaning 'sauce', is the national dish of
Mexico and there are many variations, often served with chicken or turkey.

For the mole

2 tomatoes, halved

¼ white onion, halved

½ head of garlic, sliced in half
    through the middle

2 dried ancho chillies, ribs and
    seeds removed

2 red chillies, deseeded and
    chopped

50g sesame seeds

2 tablespoons olive oil

½ teaspoon ground cinnamon

pinch ground cloves

½ teaspoon ground cumin

250ml chicken stock

2 tablespoons cacao powder

1 tablespoon fine breadcrumbs

1 tablespoon maple syrup

sea salt

To make the mole, first preheat the oven to 230°C
(450°F), Gas Mark 8.

Put the tomatoes, onion and garlic on a baking tray and
roast in the top half of the oven for 25–30 minutes.

At the same time, soak the ancho chillies in hot water.

When the roasted garlic is cool enough to handle,
squeeze the cloves out into a blender, add the other
roasted veg, softened ancho chillies and red chillies and
blend until smooth.

Toast the sesame seeds on a baking sheet for a couple of
minutes until golden. Leave to cool and then grind to a
powder in a spice mill or pestle and mortar.

Heat the oil in a large pan over a medium-high heat and
cook the ground spices for 30 seconds or so until they
release their aromas. Add the blended vegetables and
chillies, bring to a simmer and cook for about 5 minutes.

For the octopus
300g octopus tentacles
1 tablespoon olive oil

To serve
baby heritage tomatoes, halved
baby kale
red chilli, deseeded and finely
   sliced
extra virgin olive oil

Add the stock, season with a little sea salt and simmer for about 1 hour until the sauce is thickened.

Add the cacao, ground sesame seeds, breadcrumbs and maple syrup and whisk gently until incorporated. Cook for another 30 minutes, stirring occasionally. Taste and adjust the seasoning before serving.

To prepare the octopus, bring a saucepan of water to the boil and add the octopus. Simmer for 30 minutes, drain and rest for another 30 minutes. Toss the octopus tentacles in olive oil, heat a griddle pan and griddle the octopus for 3–4 minutes on each side until charred.

To serve, spread some mole over the bottom of a shallow serving dish. Toss the octopus with the tomatoes, baby kale and chilli together with some extra virgin olive oil and arrange on top of the mole. Season with a little more sea salt and serve.

◇◇◇◇◇◇

MACKEREL
WITH CACAO BLACK BEANS

This dish is packed with bold flavours to complement the
mackerel. The purée also goes very well with chicken or duck
as a side with a bit of a difference.

---

2 mackerel fillets

microgreens, to serve

lime wedges, to serve

For the beans

150g dried black beans, soaked in
    cold water overnight

½ cinnamon stick

1 bay leaf

2 garlic cloves, 1 bashed, 1 sliced

1 tablespoon olive oil

1 small red onion, sliced

¼ teaspoon mild chilli powder

1 teaspoon cumin seeds

1 teaspoon coriander seeds

75ml red wine

1 tablespoon cacao powder

1 tablespoon maple syrup

½ tablespoon cider vinegar

1 tablespoon extra virgin olive oil

sea salt

Drain the soaked black beans, rinse in cold water and
place in a large saucepan with twice their volume of
water. Add the cinnamon, bay leaf and bashed garlic
clove. Bring to the boil, then reduce to a simmer and
cook for 40–60 minutes until the beans are cooked and
soft, skimming off any foam that rises to the surface
of the water. Drain, reserving a little of the liquid, and
remove and discard the cinnamon, bay leaf and garlic
clove. Set the beans aside.

Heat the olive oil in a saucepan over a low-medium heat
and add the onion and sliced garlic clove, sautéing for
about 10 minutes. Add the chilli powder, cumin and
coriander seeds and cook for a minute before adding the
wine. Once the wine has almost disappeared, add the
cacao powder, maple syrup and vinegar, and then add
the beans into the pan.

Season with sea salt and gently mix all the ingredients
together for a minute or so.

Transfer half the beans to a blender while still warm and add the extra virgin olive oil. Blend, adding a little of the cooking liquid from the beans if needed to create a smooth purée. Heat the other half in a non-stick pan until the beans begin to pop.

Meanwhile, place a nonstick griddle pan over a high heat and place the mackerel fillets skin side down in the hot pan. Cook until the skin is crispy, about 4–5 minutes, then flip over and after a few seconds remove the pan from the heat. The fillets will finish cooking through in the residual heat.

Divide the bean purée into bowls and top with the rest of the beans and mackerel fillets. Scatter with plenty of fresh microgreens and serve with lime wedges for squeezing over.

LANGOUSTINES
WITH CACAO BUTTER

This recipe is a little bit special. Slicing the langoustines through the middle takes a little practice but as long as you use a very sharp knife and make sure you cut away from you, the end result is worth it – buttery grilled prawns that you can simply scoop out of the shells.

75ml olive oil

small pinch of crushed dried
    chillies

½ garlic clove, finely chopped

100g butter, softened

1 tablespoon pine nuts

1 tablespoon hazelnuts, chopped

1 tablespoon cacoa nibs

16 langoustines

sea salt

Preheat the grill to its highest setting.

Put the olive oil into a small saucepan, add the crushed dried chillies and garlic and gently warm over a low heat for 2–3 minutes. Remove from the heat, add the butter and leave to melt and infuse.

Heat a non-stick frying pan and add the pine nuts, chopped hazelnuts and cacao nibs, and toast for a couple of minutes. Add to the oil and butter infusion and whisk to combine.

To prepare the langoustines, hold each one firmly with your hand down on a chopping board and with the tip of the knife score a slit into the head. Then, insert the knife fully into the shell and slit the langoustine in half lengthways, making sure you cut away from your body to protect yourself.

Place the langoustines shell side down on a baking tray. Pour most of the cool, infused butter over the langoustines, season with sea salt and place under the grill for 3–5 minutes, depending on size. They will turn from translucent to a pale pinkish white when cooked.

Halfway through cooking, baste them with any remaining butter from the bowl. Serve straight away.

CACAO-CRUSTED COD

The crust in this recipe would also work well with salmon or trout fillets.
It adds a delicious crunch to the dish.

100ml vegetable stock

20g rosemary sprigs

1 tablespoon honey

1 tablespoon roasted buckwheat

½ tablespoon coconut flakes

½ tablespoon flaked almonds

½ tablespoon pumpkin seeds

½ tablespoon mixed sesame seeds

1 tablespoon cacao powder

2 x 150g cod fillets

2 tablespoons olive oil

1 teaspoon Dijon mustard

100g drained sweetcorn (or
defrosted if frozen)

2 tablespoons Greek yogurt

sea salt

rosemary flowers, to serve
(optional)

Preheat the oven to 220°C (425°F), Gas Mark 7.

Put the stock into a saucepan with the rosemary and
simmer vigorously for about 10 minutes to reduce by
about half. Whisk in the honey and then strain to
remove the rosemary; keep warm.

Prepare the crust by mixing together the buckwheat,
coconut flakes, flaked almonds, pumpkin seeds, mixed
seeds and cacao powder.

Season the cod fillets with sea salt. Heat half the olive
oil in a nonstick, ovenproof pan over a medium-high
heat. When hot, add the fillets, skin side down, and sear
for 2 minutes. Brush with mustard and top with some
of the crust mix before placing the pan in the oven to
bake for 5 minutes, or until just cooked (the time will
depend on the thickness of the fillets). Rest for a couple
of minutes.

Heat the remaining olive oil in a frying pan and sauté
the sweetcorn until slightly charred. Divide between
two shallow bowls, top with the cod fillets and gently
pour over some reduced stock. Serve with a spoonful of
Greek yogurt and a little sea salt to taste.

CATALAN CHICKEN PICADA

This is a traditional Spanish dish, which combines chocolate with Mediterranean flavours and is usually made with almonds and bread.

4 chicken legs
2 tablespoons olive oil
1 onion, finely chopped
2 garlic cloves, finely sliced
400g can chopped tomatoes
400ml chicken stock
100ml Spanish sherry
2 bay leaves
3 sprigs of thyme
sea salt and black pepper

For the picada
1 slice of stale sourdough, cubed
50g flaked almonds
30g solid cacao, chopped
pinch of ground cinnamon
pinch of ground cloves
pinch of saffron threads
¼ teaspoon fennel seeds
1 roasted black (or white) garlic
  clove
40g flat-leaf parsley
extra virgin olive oil

Season the chicken with salt and pepper while you heat the oil in a large saucepan over a medium heat. Add the chicken, skin side down and cook until the skin is browned, about 3–4 minutes on each side. Transfer to a plate and set aside.

Add the onion and garlic to the pan and cook over a medium heat for 8–10 minutes until softened. Add the chopped tomatoes and cook for a few minutes until thickened. Add the stock, sherry, bay leaves and thyme and bring to the boil. Return the chicken to the pan, season with salt and pepper, then cover and simmer over a low heat for 30 minutes, turning once during cooking.

Meanwhile, preheat the oven to 180°C (350°F), Gas Mark 4. Toast the bread cubes and almonds on a baking sheet for 8 minutes.

Add the toasted bread and almonds to a food processor with the cacao, cinnamon, ground cloves, saffron, fennel seeds, garlic, parsley and a dash of extra virgin olive oil. Process to a paste and then stir this *picada* into the sauce and simmer over low heat for 15 minutes. Rest for another 10 minutes with the lid on before serving.

PORK BELLY
WITH CACAO GLAZE

This sweet and spicy glaze cuts through the pork and adds a wonderful stickiness.
Don't stand on ceremony with this dish – put it in the middle of the table and be
prepared to move quickly.

50g honey

30ml olive oil, plus extra for
griddling

5 garlic cloves, crushed with
1 teaspoon cacao powder

2 teaspoons sea salt

½ teaspoon ground black pepper

1 dried ancho chilli (or 1 red chilli,
deseeded)

3kg boneless pork belly

2 tablespoons toasted cacao nibs
(see page 19)

Combine the honey, oil, crushed garlic and cacao, salt,
pepper and 3 tablespoons water in a small saucepan and
bring to a simmer. Add the ancho chilli, if using, and
cook until soft, about 8 minutes. Remove from the heat
and leave to cool before blending in a food processor.
If using a fresh chilli, you only need to cook for a couple
of minutes before blending.

Pour half the glaze over the pork belly and leave to
marinate at room temperature for 1 hour.

Oil a griddle pan and place over a high heat. Add the
pork and sear over a high heat for 2 minutes on each side,
then over a medium heat for 20–25 minutes, turning it
over and glazing every 10 minutes, until the meat can be
easily pierced with a knife.

Remove from the heat, place on a board and leave to rest
for 10 minutes.

Bring the remaining glaze to the boil in a small saucepan,
add the toasted cacao nibs, reduce to a low simmer and
cook for a couple of minutes until thickened. Pour the
reduced glaze over the pork and carve into slices.

VENISON
WITH CACAO YOGURT

This is Sunday lunch with a difference. Venison is a wonderfully lean and very tasty meat that works really well with the bittersweet yogurt.

For the yogurt

150g natural yogurt

1 tablespoon date syrup

1 tablespoon cacao powder

1 teaspoon sweet smoked paprika

pinch of sea salt

For the venison

1 medium venison fillet, about 500g

1 tablespoon olive oil

40g unsalted butter

5 sprigs of thyme

½ tablespoon cacao nibs

Whisk the syrup, cacao powder, paprika and salt together and fold into the yogurt. Set aside and leave the flavours to infuse while you prepare the venison.

Preheat the oven to 230°C (450°F), Gas Mark 8 while you bring the venison fillet to room temperature.

Pat the venison dry with kitchen paper and season with sea salt. Heat the oil in an ovenproof griddle pan and when hot sear the venison for 2–3 minutes on each side. Add the butter, thyme and cacao nibs to the pan and continue to cook the venison for another 2 minutes, basting with the melting butter. Give it one final baste and then place the pan in the oven for 4 minutes.

Remove from the oven and transfer the meat to a board, carefully pouring any herby butter in the pan over the meat. Cover with foil and leave to rest for 8 minutes before slicing. Serve with the cacao yogurt and plenty of fresh vegetables.

DUCK
WITH CACAO RISOTTO

The cacao in this risotto gives a lovely edge to the sweetness of
the rice, the umami mushrooms and the richness of the duck.

---

2 duck breasts

2 tablespoons olive oil, plus extra
    for the garnish

1 onion, finely chopped

3 garlic cloves, finely chopped

250g arborio rice

100g dried shiitake mushrooms,
    soaked in a small bowl of
    boiling water

1 litre hot chicken or vegetable
    stock

25g butter

1 tablespoon solid 100% cacao
    chocolate shavings

sea salt

1 small onion, sliced

Parmesan shavings, to serve

red cress or torn fresh basil,
    to serve

Preheat the oven to 160°C (325°F), Gas Mark 3.

Season the duck breasts with sea salt and place them
skin side down in an ovenproof frying pan. Place the
pan on the cold hob and turn on the heat to fairly high.
When the skin is seared and beginning to colour, turn
the breasts over and sear the other side. Turn over again
so the duck is skin side down and place in the oven to
roast for 5–8 minutes, depending on the size of the
duck breasts. You know it's done just when it has a firm
feel when pressed. Take out of the oven and rest for a
few minutes before slicing. Keep warm.

Meanwhile, start preparing the risotto. Heat the olive
oil in a large saucepan, add the onion and garlic and fry
over a low heat for about 10 minutes until soft. Add the
rice and stir to coat in the oil and onion mixture.

Slice the soaked mushrooms and add half, along with
the liquid they were soaked in, to the rice. Bring to
a simmer and stir often until the liquid has been
absorbed. Now add a ladleful of stock at a time and

simmer until absorbed; keep going until the rice
is tender. Remove from the heat and stir through
the butter and the cacao shavings.

Sauté the onion for 5 minutes in a little olive oil and
add the remaining mushrooms, sautéing for another
5 minutes.

Serve the risotto in shallow bowls topped with the duck
slices and sautéed onions and mushrooms. Season with
a little sea salt and garnish with Parmesan shavings and
cress (or basil).

BEEF SHORT RIBS
WITH CACAO AND ORANGE

Beef short ribs are inexpensive and delicious when slow cooked
with the bold flavours in this recipe.

8 beef short ribs

50g plain flour

4 streaky bacon rashers, cut into
   1cm slices

2 tablespoons olive oil

1 onion, chopped

3 celery sticks, chopped

2 shallots, finely chopped

2 garlic cloves, crushed

100ml white wine

10ml soy sauce

500ml hot chicken stock (enough
   to cover ribs)

zest and juice of 1 orange

2 bay leaves

2 sprigs of thyme

2 teaspoons Chinese five-spice
   powder

1 tablespoon soft dark brown
   sugar

1½ tablespoons cacao powder

sea salt and black pepper

Preheat the oven to 180°C (350°F), Gas Mark 4.

Season ribs with salt and pepper and then dredge in
the flour. Set aside.

In a large casserole, cook the bacon over a medium heat
until crispy and all the fat is rendered out. Remove the
bacon and set aside. Add a glug of olive oil to the bacon
grease left in the pan and increase the heat to high.
Brown the ribs on all sides, before removing and setting
aside with the bacon.

Reduce the heat to medium, add the onion, celery,
shallots and garlic and cook for 2 minutes. Add the wine
and scrape all the bits from the bottom of the pan to
make sure you keep all those flavours. Bring to the boil
and cook for a couple more minutes.

Add all the remaining ingredients and stir to combine,
then taste to check the seasoning. Return the ribs and
bacon to the pan – they should be completely covered
in liquid so add more stock if needed. Cover with the lid

To serve

1 small butternut squash,
   quartered and deseeded

2 tablespoons olive oil

1 teaspoon cumin seeds

1 teaspoon caraway seeds

3 spring onions, thinly sliced

1 red chilli, deseeded and thinly
   sliced

coriander leaves

and place in the oven for 2 hours, then reduce the heat to 160°C (325°F), Gas Mark 3 and cook for a further 30–45 minutes. The ribs should be fork-tender and beginning to fall off the bone when ready.

Meanwhile, mix the butternut squash quarters with the olive oil, cumin and caraway seeds. Tip on to a baking tray and roast in the oven for 30–40 minutes. You can put it in the oven for the last 20 minutes of the beef cooking time and then increase the oven temperature to 220°C (425°F), Gas Mark 7, for the remaining 20 minutes, or until the edges are soft and caramelized.

Remove the casserole from the oven and allow to rest for at least 20 minutes. Skim the fat off the top of the broth before serving.

Serve the beef with the roasted butternut and a scattering of sliced spring onions, chilli and coriander.

LAMB RAGU
WITH PAPPARDELLE

This dish is one of our favourites. If you only make one
recipe from the book, let it be this one.

1 tablespoon olive oil

1 onion, chopped

3 garlic cloves, crushed

2 bay leaves

2 tablespoons finely chopped
oregano

400g minced lamb

500ml lamb stock (or use chicken
stock)

1 tablespoon tomato purée

1 tablespoon cacao powder

250g dry pappardelle

150g mascarpone

20g solid 100% cacao chocolate,
finely grated

Parmesan, to serve

wild garlic shoots, to serve
(optional)

sea salt

Heat the olive oil in a large frying pan, add the onion,
garlic, bay leaves and oregano and cook, stirring, over
a medium heat for about 5 minutes. When the onion is
soft, add the lamb mince and fry until browned all over,
breaking up the lamb with a wooden spoon.

Add the stock, tomato purée and stir through the cacao
powder, bring to a simmer and cook for 30 minutes until
the liquid has reduced down.

Cook the pasta in a large pan of boiling salted water
according to the instructions on the packet. Drain and
refresh under cold running water, then tip into the
pan of lamb ragu and toss relentlessly. Finish with the
mascarpone, tossing through before serving.

Serve the pasta in a large serving bowl, with cacao
grated over, Parmesan shavings and wild garlic shoots.

BARBECUE CHICKEN

This sweet, sticky sauce is delicious brushed on chicken, burgers or vegetables on the barbecue.

---

1 tablespoon olive oil

1 onion, diced

½ teaspoon sea salt

1 tablespoon grated fresh
   root ginger

500g passata

2 tablespoons Worcestershire
   sauce

3 tablespoons runny honey

3 tablespoons blackstrap molasses

2 tablespoons cider vinegar

1 tablespoon cacao powder

1 tablespoon smoked paprika

good pinch of cayenne pepper

4 large or 8 small chicken thighs

For the barbecue sauce, heat the olive oil in a small saucepan over a medium heat and add the diced onion and the salt. Cook, stirring, for 8–10 minutes until the onion is caramelized and golden brown, then add the ginger and cook for a few more minutes.

Add all the remaining ingredients, except the chicken, and simmer until the flavours are combined, about 20 minutes.

Preheat the oven to 190°C (375°F), Gas Mark 5.

Marinate the chicken thighs in 4–6 tablespoons of the barbecue sauce in a bowl for 20–30 minutes. Place in an oven dish and bake in the oven for about 30 minutes. Alternatively, cook on a hot barbecue grill.

Serve with Cardamom Roasted Sweet Potato (*see* page 64, if liked).

ONGLET
WITH MISO CACAO BUTTER

Onglet is a type of steak that is less expensive than rib-eye or sirloin but with
a bit of care and attention is just as tender. The miso cacao butter adds
a wonderful umami flavour.

400g onglet steak
1 teaspoon white miso
1 teaspoon cacao powder
1 tablespoon olive oil
30g unsalted butter
sea salt

Bring the steak to room temperature and season with a
little salt. Mix together the miso and cacao.

Place a griddle pan over a high heat and add the olive
oil. When it is very hot, add the steak and sear for
3–4 minutes on each side, turning quite often as onglet
is more tender when cooked in this way, rather than
leaving for a few minutes before turning.

Remove from the heat and add the butter and the miso
cacao mixture, spooning it over the onglet as it melts.
Rest for 8 minutes before removing from the pan to slice.
Then heat up the butter again in the pan and add the
steak slices back to the pan just to heat through.

Serve with your favourite vegetables or a green salad.

SWEETS

CACAO CHIA PAN BROWNIE

Brownies are one of the easiest cakes to bake – perfect for those times when you just need a chocolaty treat. We've added chia seeds into the mix, although we have to admit the butter and sugar mean this isn't the healthiest recipe, but we couldn't resist including it.

120g butter, plus extra for greasing
250g coconut sugar
80g cacao powder
45g self-raising flour
¼ teaspoon sea salt
1 teaspoon vanilla extract
2 large eggs
40g chia seeds
1 tablespoon dried rose petals, to serve (optional)
1 tablespoon lime zest, to serve (optional)

Preheat the oven to 160°C (325°F), Gas Mark 3 and line a 20cm square brownie tin with baking paper or butter a nonstick pan (as pictured).

Melt the butter in a saucepan until it darkens in colour and smells nutty.

Mix together the sugar, cacao powder, flour and salt in a large bowl, then slowly pour in the melted butter, whisking to blend. Add the vanilla extract, then whisk in the eggs. Stir in the chia seeds until just combined, and then pour the mixture into the prepared tin.

Bake for 20 minutes, or until a skewer comes out with just a few moist crumbs attached and cracks form across the top. Leave to cool before removing from the tin, scattering over dried rose petals and lime zest, if using, and cutting into squares or slices.

HOMEMADE CHOCOLATE BARS

This is a very easy way of making homemade chocolate, which is just
about the perfect holiday or birthday gift. To make these bars, you
need a silicone chocolate bar mould, available online or in baking
shops. Be creative with the toppings – what do you fancy?

4 tablespoons cacao butter
1 tablespoon coconut oil
3 tablespoons cacao powder
2 tablespoons agave syrup
1 teaspoon vanilla extract
pinch of sea salt

Topping options
dried edible flowers
Himalayan salt
freeze-dried raspberries
chopped nuts
cacao nibs

Melt the cacao butter and coconut oil in a bain-marie:
set a heatproof bowl over a small saucepan of barely
simmering water, making sure the base of the bowl
doesn't touch the water. When it is completely liquid,
stir in the cacao powder, followed by the agave syrup,
vanilla and salt. Stir until all the ingredients are
thoroughly combined and you have a silky texture.

Pour the mixture into your moulds of choice and
sprinkle over your chosen toppings. Place in the freezer
for 1 hour to set, then remove from the moulds and wrap
in greaseproof paper. Store in the refrigerator for up to
4 months.

BLACK SESAME SNAPS

These make a wonderful snack. You don't need to use black sesame seeds if you only
have white to hand, although they look amazing. Sesame seeds are a rich source of
healthy fats, which is why they work well as an energy snack.

200g black sesame seeds
100g runny honey, plus
    1 tablespoon
2 tablespoons coconut milk
sea salt
50g solid 100% cacao chocolate

Preheat the oven to 180°C (350°F), Gas Mark 4 and grease
and line a baking sheet with baking paper.

Mix together the sesame seeds, honey, 1 tablespoon of the
coconut milk and a pinch of sea salt. Tip the mixture on
to the lined baking sheet and flatten out with the back
of a spoon, noting that it will spread a little more in the
oven. Bake for 5–7 minutes. Leave to cool and then break
into snack-sized pieces.

Meanwhile, melt the solid cacao chocolate in a bain-
marie: put into a heatproof bowl with the remaining
tablespoon of coconut milk and set over a pan of barely
simmering water, making sure the base of the bowl
doesn't touch the water. Take off the heat and stir
through the remaining honey.

Dip the sesame snaps into the melted cacao and place
on the now cool lined baking tray. Cool the snaps in the
refrigerator to solidify the chocolate, then transfer to an
airtight container and keep for up to a week.

DEEP-FRIED CACAO RAVIOLI

Ravioli might not immediately come to mind as a dessert,
but the combination of orange zest, cacao, creamy ricotta
and honey turn these pasta parcels into moreish bites.

3 eggs, beaten
240g '00' or plain flour, plus extra
   for dusting
1 tablespoon extra virgin olive oil
1 teaspoon sea salt
125g ricotta
zest of ½ orange
1 tablespoon cacao powder
1 egg white, beaten
vegetable oil, for frying

To serve
honeycomb, or honey
Greek yogurt
cranberries or raspberries

Mix the eggs, flour, extra virgin olive oil and salt in a large
bowl with your hands or in the bowl of a food mixer
until a dough forms. Continue to knead by hand or with
the dough hook attachment of the mixer until the dough
is smooth and elastic, about 10 minutes. Wrap the dough
in clingfilm, and place in the refrigerator for 30 minutes.

Meanwhile, combine the ricotta, orange zest and cacao
in a small bowl and set aside.

Lightly dust a pasta machine and cut your pasta dough
into four equal pieces. Starting at the widest setting,
roll the dough through the machine. Fold the pasta in
half, and roll the dough through the same setting one
more time before repeating at the next setting. Continue
rolling the dough until you get to the thinnest setting to
create four thin sheets of pasta.

Place teaspoonfuls of the ricotta mix at 6cm intervals
along the bottom edge of each sheet. Brush the egg white
around the ricotta and fold the top half over the bottom

half, enclosing the ricotta. Cut the ravioli with a sharp knife or a serrated pastry cutter. You can chill the ravioli at this stage until ready to cook.

When you are ready to cook the ravioli, fill a saucepan with oil to about 5cm deep and use a kitchen thermometer to heat the oil to 180°C (350°F). If you don't have a thermometer you can test the oil by dropping in a small scrap of pasta dough; it should sizzle when it hits the oil. Add the ravioli in batches, cooking for 3 minutes until they are a light golden colour. Remove with a slotted spoon and drain on kitchen paper.

Serve with Greek yogurt, honeycomb and cranberries or raspberries.

PANCAKES
WITH MELTED CACAO

This is a really simple crowd-pleaser of a dessert or Sunday morning treat. When combined with the cacao chocolate the butter works a little bit like cocoa butter to soften the bitterness. Similarly, the maple syrup adds a little natural sweetness.

250g gram (chickpea) flour
2 pinches of sea salt
coconut oil, for frying

To serve
butter
80g solid 100% cacao chocolate,
    roughly broken into pieces
maple syrup
ground cinnamon, chilli flakes or
    crushed pink peppercorns
sea salt

To make the pancakes, put the flour into a large bowl and stir through a good pinch of salt. Make a well in the middle and slowly pour in 400ml water, whisking all the time, until you have a smooth batter. Set aside for at least 30 minutes at room temperature (even better, make this the night before).

To cook the pancakes, heat a little coconut oil in a nonstick frying pan. When nice and hot, ladle enough batter into the pan to make the pancake size of your choice. Cook for a couple of minutes and then flip over to cook for the same amount of time on the other side. Place on a hot serving plate and immediately add a knob of butter, a few pieces of chocolate and a generous drizzle of maple syrup. Repeat with the remaining batter, until all used up.

To serve, sprinkle cinnamon, chilli or crushed pink peppercorns over the melting butter and cacao and finish with a few sea salt flakes.

MAKES 20 PIECES

◇◇◇◇◇◇

SALAME DE CHOCOLATE

Similar to rocky road, *salame de chocolate* is popular in Portugal and is very easy to make. We have added some dried cherries to the traditional recipe and replaced the plain biscuits with ginger biscuits.

25g flaked almonds
25g pistachios, chopped
150g unsalted butter
6 tablespoons coconut sugar
2 egg yolks
2 tablespoons cacao powder
200g dark chocolate chips
150g ginger biscuits, roughly broken
50g dried cherries
1 tablespoon icing sugar (optional)

Preheat the oven to 180°C (350°F), Gas Mark 4.

Place the almonds and pistachios on a baking sheet and toast in the oven for about 7 minutes. Remove from the oven and tip into a bowl to cool.

Melt the butter in a saucepan over a low heat. Remove from the heat and stir in the coconut sugar, egg yolks, cacao powder and chocolate chips. Return to a low heat and stir continuously until all the ingredients are melted and combined to a smooth consistency.

Pour the chocolate mixture into the bowl with the toasted almonds and pistachios and mix thoroughly. Add the ginger biscuits and cherries, and stir to combine, then chill in the refrigerator for about 15 minutes.

Tip the chilled chocolate mixture on to a sheet of greaseproof paper and mould it into a cylinder shape. Roll the paper tightly around the mixture and twist the ends, then roll the log on an even surface to create a smooth, salami-type shape. Chill for about 4 hours.

Remove from the refrigerator and unwrap the chocolate salami from the baking paper. Dust with icing sugar, if using, and slice off pieces to serve. Wrap up again in the greaseproof paper to store in the refrigerator for up to 7 days.

BRAZILIAN BRIGADEIRO

These traditional Brazilian sweets are simply cacao, butter and condensed milk, so they are definitely not a sugar-free treat, but you do only need one small truffle to feel like you are indulging yourself!

3 tablespoons unsalted butter, plus extra for greasing

400g can sweetened condensed milk

pinch of sea salt

4 tablespoons cacao powder

1 teaspoon vanilla extract

To decorate

chopped pistachios

desiccated coconut

cacao powder

cacao nibs

Lightly grease a large plate.

Put the butter, condensed milk, salt and cacao powder into a heavy-based saucepan and place over a medium heat. Bring slowly to the boil, stirring constantly with a wooden spoon. Reduce the heat to medium-low and cook for 10–15 minutes, stirring constantly, until the mixture is thick and shiny and starts to pull away from the bottom of the pan.

Stir in the vanilla and vigorously mix again. Pour the mixture on to the greased plate and chill in the refrigerator for at least 2 hours.

Butter your hands and pinch off some of the dough to make walnut-sized balls. Place your coating ingredients into small bowls and roll the balls in one of the bowls. Place in mini paper cases or on a tray lined with nonstick baking paper.

Store in the refrigerator for up to 10 days.

RAW CACAO
AND BLACK BEAN MOUSSE

At first glance you might be forgiven for thinking this recipe sounds pretty
strange: black bean mousse? But we promise you won't taste the beans; they
simply help create a fluffy consistency. Try them, you won't regret it! This is a
dessert with no guilt attached.

200g canned black beans, drained
    and rinsed
½ teaspoon ground cinnamon
6 medjool dates, pitted
1 tablespoon coconut oil
1 tablespoon cashew nut butter
½ teaspoon vanilla extract
80ml cashew nut milk
100g solid 100% cacao chocolate

In a food processor, blend together the black beans,
cinnamon, dates, coconut oil, cashew nut butter, vanilla
and a little of the cashew nut milk until smooth.

Melt the chocolate in a bain-marie: set a heatproof bowl
with the remaining cashew nut milk over a saucepan
of barely simmering water, making sure the base of the
bowl doesn't touch the water. Whisk until smooth.

Leave the chocolate mixture to cool for a minute and
then add to the ingredients in the food processor and
blend until smooth.

Divide the mixture into individual glass jars or serving
dishes and chill in the refrigerator for at least 3 hours
before serving.

CACAO BUTTER FUDGE

This isn't a traditional fudge recipe but it is smooth and chocolaty and, yes, you could definitely mistake it for fudge.

250g maple syrup
180g raw cacao butter, chopped
80g extra virgin coconut oil
125g coconut butter
1 teaspoon vanilla extract
pinch of sea salt
zest of 1 lime

Line a loaf tin with baking paper.

Put the maple syrup into a small saucepan and bring it to a simmer over a medium heat. Cook for a few minutes, stirring occasionally, until it has reduced in volume by about half. Set aside.

Meanwhile, put the cacao butter, coconut oil and coconut butter into a heatproof bowl and set over a small saucepan of simmering water, making sure the base of the bowl doesn't touch the water. Melt together until smooth. Remove from the heat and add the thickened maple syrup, vanilla and salt, stirring to thoroughly combine.

Pour this into the lined tin, sprinkle over the lime zest and chill in the refrigerator for 2–3 hours until set. Once set, turn out of the pan and cut into cubes.

Store in the refrigerator for up to 10 days.

CACAO BEETROOT CAKE

Chocolate and beetroot are a match made in heaven, and this dark, almost flourless cake is an intense treat that actually contains lots of goodness.

250g solid 100% cacao chocolate, roughly chopped

3 large eggs

200g light muscovado sugar

100g self-raising flour

½ teaspoon bicarbonate of soda

½ teaspoon baking powder

pinch of sea salt

50g ground almonds

250g raw beetroot, peeled and grated

75ml sunflower oil

50ml avocado oil

For the topping

1 avocado

40g cacao powder

150g maple syrup

1 teaspoon rose water

Preheat the oven to 140°C (275°CF), Gas Mark 1 and grease a 20cm loose-bottomed cake tin. Line the bottom with baking paper.

Melt the chocolate in a bain-marie: place it into a heatproof bowl and set the bowl over a small saucepan of simmering water, making sure the base of the bowl doesn't touch the water. Stir until smooth, then set aside to cool.

Using a hand-held electric mixer, beat the eggs with the sugar in a large bowl until pale and fluffy. Fold in the flour, bicarbonate of soda, baking powder, salt, cacao powder and ground almonds until thoroughly mixed together. Now fold in the beetroot, melted chocolate and oils until evenly combined.

Pour the batter into the prepared tin and bake for 30 minutes in the centre of the oven. Cover the cake with foil and return to the oven for another 30 minutes. Turn out of the tin and leave to cool on a wire rack.

For the filling

400g black seedless grapes, on the vine

1 tablespoon olive oil

250g Greek yogurt, strained through muslin

To make the topping, put the avocado, cacao powder, maple syrup and rose water in a food processor and process until smooth.

To roast the grapes for the filling, preheat the oven to 220°C (425°CF), Gas Mark 7. Toss in a little olive oil and roast for about 30 minutes until caramelized. Leave to cool and slice about half the grapes, keeping the rest to garnish the cake.

Slice the cake into two discs. Spread the strained yogurt over the bottom half and add the halved grapes evenly. Top with the other half of the cake and spread over the cacao ganache topping. Arrange the roasted grapes on the vine to serve.

MAKES 12

◇◇◇◇◇◇

PEANUT BUTTER CACAO CUPS

These individual cups are a real treat, but the sweetness comes from honey or maple syrup instead of sugar, so they are an excellent alternative to most shop-bought chocolates or sweet treats. They are also incredibly filling, so you won't be tempted to eat the whole batch.

100g coconut oil, melted

40g cacao powder

½ teaspoon vanilla extract

2 tablespoon raw honey or pure maple syrup

pinch of sea salt, plus extra for topping

raw peanut butter or almond butter (stir well and chill in the refrigerator ahead of time)

Mix the coconut oil, cacao powder, vanilla, honey or maple syrup and sea salt together in a bowl. Pour a small amount of this chocolate mixture, about 2 teaspoons, into mini paper baking cases. Place these on a small tray and transfer to the freezer for 5 minutes to make the chocolate firm.

Remove the tray from the freezer and spoon a small dollop of peanut butter in the centre of each cup. Add more of the chocolate mixture to each cup until filled to the top. Return to the freezer for another 5–10 minutes until the chocolate has set solid. Sprinkle over a few sea salt flakes.

Store in the refrigerator for up to 10 days.

STICKY RICE PUDDING
WITH MANGO

This is a stovetop rice pudding to die for. If you are feeling more saintly than us,
swap the double cream for Greek yogurt.

50g short-grain rice

100ml coconut milk

1 tablespoon agave nectar or
    coconut syrup

zest of 1 orange

1 tablespoon cacao powder

1 vanilla pod, split lengthways and
    seeds scraped a little

50ml double cream

zest of a lime

squeeze of lime

1 ripe mango, diced

cacao nibs, to serve

Put the rice, coconut milk, agave or coconut syrup,
orange zest, cacao powder and vanilla pod (with seeds)
into a saucepan and bring to the boil over a medium
heat. Reduce the heat and simmer until the rice is
cooked, about 30 minutes, stirring often to prevent it
sticking to the bottom of the pan. Take off the heat and
leave to cool for a few minutes before stirring through
the cream.

Serve the rice pudding warm or chilled with the lime
zest and juice, mango and cacao nibs.

CACAO AND LEMONGRASS ICE CREAM

The lime leaves and lemongrass add a tart freshness alongside the dark cacao, while the chocolate soil adds the perfect crunch with a wonderful bitter edge.

500ml whole milk

150g caster sugar

2 heaped tablespoons cacao powder

6 kaffir lime leaves, fresh or dried

1 lemongrass stalk, bashed

4 egg yolks

For the chocolate soil

30g plain flour

30g cacao powder

30g coconut sugar

pinch sea salt

40g unsalted butter, melted

Pour the milk into a saucepan, add half the sugar, place over a high heat and bring just to the boil. Remove the pan from the heat. In a bowl, make a paste with some of the hot sweet milk and the cacao powder. Whisk this into the hot milk. Add the lime leaves and lemongrass stalk to the pan and leave to infuse, with the lid on, until the mixture is cold.

Using an electric whisk, beat the egg yolks with the remaining sugar until combined and creamy. On a low setting, slowly add the cooled milk (with lemongrass and lime leaves removed). Once fully combined, pour back into the pan and heat gently, stirring continuously, until thickened.

Chill for an hour, stirring every now and then, before churning for about 30 minutes to reach a soft serve consistency. If freezing, transfer to a suitable container, and leave to soften for 15 minutes before serving.

For the chocolate soil, preheat the oven to 160°C (320°F), Gas Mark 3 and line a baking tray with baking paper. Mix together the flour, cacao powder, coconut sugar and salt. Pour in the melted butter and mix together. Spread out over the lined tray and bake for 15 minutes. Set aside and cool before using.

BEAUTY

FACE MASK

Cacao is rich in antioxidants called flavonoids, which aren't just good for us to include in our daily diet, but are also great for the skin, stimulating circulation and smoothing fine lines. Antioxidants are essential anti-agers, fighting free radical damage and repairing skin cells. Cacao is also anti-inflammatory, so can help to soothe redness and reduce skin blemishes. This simple face mask combines cacao with clay, which helps to draw out toxins and protect and nourish the skin with its rich mineral content.

---

1 tablespoon raw cacao powder
1 teaspoon bentonite clay powder
    (available online)
½ teaspoon avocado oil
diluted cider vinegar
    (1 tablespoon cider vinegar
    to 5 tablespoons water)

Stir the cacao powder and bentonite clay powder together with a non-metallic spoon. Mix in the oil and then add a tablespoon of diluted cider vinegar at a time until you reach a creamy, paste-like consistency.

Apply in a thick layer over cleansed skin, avoiding the eyes, and leave for 10 minutes.

Use an old face cloth to remove the mask as it will stain – simply soak in hand-hot water, squeeze out the water and then hold against your face to feel the warmth for a couple of seconds before gently wiping away the mask. Repeat until all the mask is removed and then rinse your face with cool water and pat dry.

Apply a little facial oil or moisturizer.

BODY BUTTER

In warmer climates, you might need to keep this body butter in the
refrigerator to prevent it from melting. You can also reduce the amount of
coconut oil in warmer seasons and use 40 drops of a favourite essential oil as
an alternative to the vanilla extract. When you use this body butter it melts
very quickly on the skin and at first appears to be very oily, but oils are quickly
absorbed and it is intensely moisturizing.

80g raw cacao butter
60g coconut oil
1 teaspoon vanilla extract

Melt the cacao butter in a bain-marie: place in a
heatproof bowl set over a pan of gently simmering
water, making sure the base of the bowl doesn't touch
the water. Stir in the coconut oil until the mixture is
completely liquid.

Remove from the heat, stir in the vanilla extract (or
essential oil) and leave to cool for about 10 minutes.
Chill in the refrigerator for about 45 minutes until
the mixture begins to solidify (or about 10 minutes
in the freezer). The mixture will change from a clear
appearance to opaque.

Use a hand-held blender to whisk the mixture. Leave
for 30 minutes until it becomes fairly solid in texture
and work into a cylinder shape. Use greaseproof paper
to wrap around the 'butter' and smooth the shape.
Transfer to an airtight container and keep for up to
4 months. You can then slice off discs to use.

◇◇◇◇◇◇

BODY SCRUB

This body scrub is a delicious way to exfoliate your skin with the grainy sugar and relieve dryness with the avocado oil and anti-inflammatory cacao. Natural body scrubs also make beautiful presents when presented in mason jars.

200g granulated or coconut sugar

35g cacao powder

1 teaspoon vanilla extract

2 tablespoons avocado oil

Combine the sugar and cacao powder in a mixing bowl. Add the rest of the ingredients and mix until thoroughly combined. Transfer to a wide-rimmed airtight container.

To use in the shower, step aside from the water flow, scoop the scrub out of the jar and apply to damp skin, paying attention to feet and elbows. Rinse off in the shower.

FOOT CREAM

With its combination of essential oils this foot cream will wake up
tired feet and moisturize and soothe away the day.

50g shea butter

25g raw cacao butter

20 drops of rosemary essential oil

20 drops of peppermint essential
oil

10 drops of lavender essential oil

10 drops of tea tree essential oil

Put the shea and cacao butters into a heatproof bowl
and set over a small saucepan of gently simmering
water, making sure the base of the bowl doesn't touch
the water. Melt until the mixture is fully liquid.

Leave to cool for 10 minutes, stir through the essential
oils, then cover the bowl and transfer to the freezer
to chill for about 10–15 minutes until solid, but not
too hard.

Blend using a hand-held blender until soft and whipped
in texture. Transfer to a wide-rimmed airtight jar.

To use, simply scoop out a small amount of cream and
indulge your feet.

CARDAMOM CACAO BATH MILK

Adding milk to a bath is a wonderful way to turn a bath into a ritual, and it's also really good for softening and renewing your skin. Both silk powder and coconut milk powder are a little unusual but are easily available to purchase online. Silk powder is used to create a softer texture.

30g raw cacao butter

½ teaspoon silk powder

8 heaped tablespoons coconut milk powder

1 tablespoon rose water

1 teaspoon ground cardamom

Combine the cacao butter, silk powder, half the coconut milk powder and rose water in a small food processor or spice mill and grind until fine. It will be a little pasty to touch.

Scrape out into a bowl and add the remaining coconut milk powder, mixing and breaking up any clumps to make it as powdery as you can. Add the ground cardamom and combine thoroughly. Transfer to an airtight glass jar.

To use, add a generous sprinkle to a hot bath or foot bath, swirling to dissolve in the water.

INDEX

◇◇◇◇◇◇